Beautiful Trees
For Kids!

Nature Books for Kids
By
K. Bennett

JD-Biz Publishing

Read More Amazing Animal Books

Purchase at Amazon.com

Table of Contents

Introduction

You will find something more in woods than in books. Trees and stones will teach you that which you can never learn from masters.
~Saint Bernard

***

Trees: Trees are beautiful plants made of wood with strong roots, pretty green leaves, and occasionally yummy fruit! They are fun to climb, explore, and learn about.

Lots of interesting creatures live inside the bark of trees and some live in the branches. Other animals dig a hole under the tree and live there too!

The roots of a tree do more than just keep it standing tall. Roots are like a beehive for creatures in the earth! Roots also give water to the tree and the nutrients it needs.

What do you know about trees?

Some trees live for thousands of years and some grow very tall and wide. Think of the Sequoia tree. This is a "King" among trees. It can be as tall as a 26 story building!

The wood from trees has been used for a very long time to help humans. Do you know how we use the wood from trees?

- *For Energy:* Building a fire to keep warm or scare away bad animals. Many people have fireplaces in their homes and some people still cook with firewood.

- *In Construction*: Many homes are made of wood and many floors are too!

- *For Furniture:* Did you ever see a pretty wood table or chairs? What about a head board?

*- **For Decoration:*** Do you like picture or painting frames made of wood? What about vases, souvenirs, plates, or nicely painted bowls?

*- **To make paper:*** Yes, paper comes from the chips and sawdust of trees! Toilet paper comes from trees also.

*- **For Games:*** Board games and other types of games are made from wood and many children toys are made of wood.

*- **For Cleaning Supplies:*** Shampoos, shoe polish, and even cleaning supplies for the home, comes from a tree!

This list is just a small sample of what trees can do. Did you know the wood of trees is used for thousands of products?

How many other things can you add to this list?

Trees come in all shapes and sizes but if a tree is small it is called a shrub instead of a tree. Do you know how many trees are in the world?

I will give you three guesses to choose from:

1- **100,000,000** (One hundred million)

2- **250,676,250** (Two hundred fifty million, six hundred seventy-six thousand, two hundred fifty) Whew! What a lot of words!

3- **400,246,300,201** (Four hundred billion, two hundred forty six million, three hundred thousand, two hundred one.)

Which number did you choose?

If you said **number 3**, you are correct! Think of it like this: For every 61 trees on this planet, there is 1 person!

Are you wondering how we know the number of the trees? Can you guess?

Satellites help us to count the number of trees. And the satellites from NASA in 2008 said there were around 61 trees for every human being on the planet. Pretty amazing, don't you think?

What about today? The number is still over **400** billion trees! But this number can change. Why?

Well, it depends on how many new trees are planted and how many trees are cut down to make different things.

Can you guess how many trees are cut down each day?

*80,000 – 160,000 trees per day!

That's a lot of trees! And every year we lose **60,000** square kilometers (23,166 square miles) of trees around the world.

Are you thinking…'we have billions of trees so a few thousand don't really matter?' Is this true?

Let's see how important trees really are and then come up with your own conclusions. Don't forget to share your findings with others.

Remember: Sharing is Caring!

DID YOU KNOW?

There are two main types of trees. Those that lose their leaves during the changing seasons and those that keep their leaves green all year long.

- The ones that lose their leaves are called: **Deciduous.**
- The ones that stay green all the time are called: **Evergreen.**

Evergreen trees do lose leaves from time to time but it always makes new leaves before the old ones fall off! This is how it can stay green all the time.

Which one do you like best? Explain your reasons to a friend, classmate or your parents.

Chapter 1
Let's learn more!

Ok Explorer, let's dig in and learn about the components of a tree:

Roots: Roots go deep into the ground and help to feed the tree. There are lots of roots in a tree. Many times the size of the tree on top tells you how big the roots are below!

Roots help the tree to stand strong. If the tree did not have good, solid roots it could tip over! Roots also help the tree get water and the nutrients it needs to be strong and healthy.
Without good roots, the tree will not be strong or healthy.

Branches: The branches of a tree help to hold the leaves. Imagine if the tree had no branches! Where would the leaves be? Do you like branches? So do I!

Branches help the tree to get the water it needs and it stores extra sugar too.

Leaves: The leaves of a tree are not only pretty but very important. They use the energy to make food or sugar that the tree needs to "eat." How does it happen? By a process called photosynthesis.

Crown: Did you think of a king or queen with a crown? Where do they wear it? On their heads? Great job! A tree is the same way. The crown includes the leaves and the branches at the very top of the tree.

Did you know a tree's crown is better than a crown full of jewels? Why do we say that? Because a jeweled crown does not shade a person's head from the sun, right? But a tree's crown protects the roots with a nice shade so the hot sun doesn't burn them all up!

The crown also helps the tree to stay cool by a process called "transpiration." Don't worry! I will explain at the end of the book what this process is all about.

Bark: This is the outside part of the trunk and it protects the soft wood inside the tree.

Cambium: After you get past the bark, the layer on the other side is called Cambium. It's alive! Why do we say that? Because it's a cell factory that helps the tree to grow wider from year to year!

Sapwood: This part of the tree is alive too and has a pretty, light color! This helps the nutrients and water to get from the roots to the branches. Sapwood is very young but when the years go by and it gets older and older, then it becomes heartwood. Isn't that a beautiful name?

Heartwood: This part of the tree is darker than Sapwood because it is much older. It is in the center of the tree and makes it nice and strong. It is the "hardest" wood in the tree.

Pith: This part of the tree has really neat sponge like cells. It helps the tree to get the nutrients from one place to another and it sits right in the center of the tree!

Trunk: The trunk holds the tree in place and helps it stay strong. The trunk also helps the nutrients and water get where it needs to go. Did you know the trunk is very good at keeping a secret? What kind of secret do you think I am talking about? Can you guess?

What's the best way to tell the age of a tree? I'll give you a few options:

1- Ask the tree how old it is.

2- Throw the leaves in a river and see if they float, the number of leaves that do, is the trees age.

3- Count the roots, be sure to dig all around the base of the tree, roots are everywhere.

4- Count the number of branches.

5- Count the rings inside the trunk.

Pick one!

Did you choose a number? Which number did you choose? **Was it 5**? Great job!

The rings of a tree reveal how old the tree really is. Each year a new ring is added so many people call them "annual" rings.

DID YOU KNOW?

Some people study trees but some go even deeper than that! Did you know there is a branch of science that studies the rings of the trees?

They are called **Dendrochronologists**. What a big word!

This type of studies helps scientists to read the "story" of a tree. Yes! Trees are great storytellers and help us to understand what is happening around us.

What kind of stories do you think trees tell us?

Sometimes a tree will "tell" you if too much rain fell and a flood happened. Or they might "talk" about earthquakes and droughts. Some of them "talk" about insect infestations, lightning strikes, and much more!

But how does a tree "talk" without saying a word?

Scientists examine how thick or thin a ring is. And then they guess what happened around it.

For example, if a ring is really thick scientists say the tree grew healthy and strong! So this means, the tree got enough sunlight, food, and water.

Sometimes the rings will be very thin. When they see this, scientists say something happened during the growing process of the tree. This could be bad conditions, drought, or even disease!

(Source: *Realtrees4kids.org and kidzone.ws/plants/trees.html*)

Did you enjoy learning about the components of a tree? Wonderful!
Now comes the fun part! Let's talk about some very special trees and
how important they are.

Chapter 2
Trees are wonderful!

Coconut Tree

This tree is very famous for lots of reasons! You might know about the fruit or maybe you think of it on tropical islands with lots of white sand. But there is much more to a coconut tree than meets the eye!

What makes Coconut trees so special?

Let's learn more!

Coconut palm is *Cocos Nucifera* and it is family to the palm tree. Think of them like cousins that look a lot alike!

The word actually comes from the the word "**Cocos**" in Spanish and Portuguese and it means "grinning face!"

If you look at a coconut carefully, can you see three small holes that look like a laughing face?

Coconut can be used in many, many different ways and every part of the tree has something great to offer. For this book, we will focus on the coconut fruit and water in the fruit.

To start with, a coconut is a ***drupe*** with three layers like a typical fruit. But unlike other fruit, a coconut is a nut, a fruit, and a seed all in the same casing!

What an amazing tree to produce such a fascinating fruit!

QUICK FUN FACTS!

A coconut tree can be used in the following amazing ways…

For: *Milk, Oil, Makeup, Lotions, Alcoholic drinks, Canoes, Furniture, Drums, Containers, Fuel, Charcoal, Copra, and much more!*

And in many parts of the world, people use monkeys to help them get the coconuts!

Sequoia and Redwood Trees

These trees are the "Kings" of trees as we said before. They are not only very tall, but also very wide. They are called "nature's skyscrapers" because they grow very high into the sky!

If you were to stand below one of these amazing trees, you will feel very small!

A very famous sequoia called **General Sherman** is about more than 250 feet tall and his waist is 102 feet wide. Can you guess how much he weighs? More than 2 million pounds! How much do you weigh?

Redwoods are other amazing trees that grow hundreds of feet into the air. They also live for thousands of years and have been on planet earth for millions of years. They are very ancient trees.

Hyperion is a well-known Redwood that stands at more than 370 feet high! Something really amazing about Redwoods is how they can make their own rain if they need it.

How do they make rain?

Redwoods catch fog and hold it in their leaves and branches. This moisture helps the tree to get the nutrients it needs and grow healthy and strong.

What a smart tree!

Apple Trees

Apples trees are very special trees with an amazing fruit! Each year millions and millions of apples are sold around the world and many people enjoy them! What is your favorite apple? Red, green, yellow? How do you like to eat them?

There are many different types of apples with cute names like: Pink Lady, Granny Smith, Fuji, Gala, Red delicious, Golden delicious and many more.

Have you heard of the saying "***An apple a day keeps the doctor away***?" Many people believe if you eat an apple a day, you will have good health. What about you? Do you agree with them?

Why are apples so good to eat? Why don't you research this question and see what you can find. Then come up with your own conclusions and share your findings with others!

Chapter 3
More Fun facts!

Now let's talk about some cool tree facts you may or may not know about!

Trees help us with the environment and they help to keep things cool. Have you heard of climate change? Do you know what this means? In our book "*Beautiful Seasons for Kids*" we talked a little about it:

Climate change: is something we are still learning about, but it can affect the seasons in many ways. For example, the rains may last longer or it may not rain at all. The days might get hotter or colder and the winds might be stronger than before.

How do trees help with climate change?

Trees help in lots of different ways. In some places they help the rain to fall more often! They help with fog too. Do you remember which trees hold fog in their leaves? Good memory!

Trees help us when it gets too hot with their big, beautiful leaves. They give us shade and block out the burning sun.

Around the roots of trees in the forest, the water that comes down from rain and snow stays there. This neat skill helps with drought, because if there is no rain for a long time the trees can soak up the water left behind from the rain and snow!

Trees are great places for creatures to live! Can you think of animals that love to live in trees? Here are some I thought of: squirrels, sloths, monkeys, tree frogs (Yes, frogs live in trees too!), many birds (They love to build their nest on the branches of trees), and lots of bugs!

I know you can add lots of other creatures to this list. Have fun with your research.

When the leaves die they fall on the forest floor. Then they decompose and soak into the ground over time. This process is very important! Do you know why?

Maybe you think dead leaves are just trash. Not with trees! The dead leaves help many other things to keep living and growing too! Things like microorganisms, some species of worm, mushrooms, and other plants.

FUN ACTIVITY!

This activity is adapted from ***reachoutmichigan.org***. The goal is to improve our learning and our sense of discovery. So, let's be junior scientists! For this project you will need:

-Paper to write on

-Pencils, crayons, or whatever you want to write with

- A cushion or something to sit on

- Something to hold your supplies

-A snack

- Water to drink

-A little time to explore!

Are you ready? Here is your assignment…

Look at different trees and try to figure out what type of tree it is! Is it a deciduous tree or evergreen? If you don't know what kinds of trees are deciduous trees, here are of few of the most common: maple, oak, birch, elm, and hickory.

All of these trees are deciduous trees. Do you remember what deciduous means? Yes! This means it will lose it leaves during the year. And Evergreen means the tree stays green all year long. Some types of Evergreens are: pine (There are many kinds!), cedar, blue spruce, and juniper.

If you don't know what these trees look like, ask your parent's or a guardian's permission to search online for the pictures!

And finally: I promised to explain the process of **transpiration** at the beginning of the book? You didn't forget, did you?

Answer: Start at the bottom of the tree where the roots go deep in the ground. The water travels up the bark, then to the branches and all the way out to the leaves. When the water gets to the leaves, it heats up with the sun. Then the sun evaporates the water and passes through the little holes or pores of the leaf and vanishes into the air!

And that's the process of transpiration!

Conclusion:

In conclusion: Learning about trees is a fascinating adventure! Would you like to continue learning a little more about them?

A creative idea for you!

Pick a tree, any tree, and ask yourself what makes it different from other trees. Then think about the best way to protect it. If you were in charge, what would you do to keep the tree safe?

More Ideas:

There are lots of interesting animals that live around trees. Pick one and decide why you like it so much. Maybe you can use this creature for show and tell or for your school project. Don't forget to share your findings with your schoolmates and your teacher. Or you may decide to share it with your family, instead of at school.

If you don't know which creature to choose, do some research and find something exciting to talk about.

For example: How are flying squirrels different than other squirrels. Do they eat the fruit from the trees? Where do they sleep? How do they take care of their little babies? What kind of trees do they live in? Deciduous or Evergreen?

Another, fun activity:

This activity is listed at *Kidspot.com.au* and it is a game you can enjoy playing with friends and family. It will help you to see how good you are at remembering things and how much you love to "hug-a-tree!"

To play this game you need to be a place with lots of trees. You might like to play in a park or near a forest. Remember to choose a safe place to play the game.

Ready?

First you need to set a starting point. This is your home base where you will start the game. Then you need to split into pairs and one of you will be blindfolded.

Your partner will take you to a tree and you have to feel the bark, branches, or the leaves. Try to sniff so you know what it smells like. Touch it with your fingers so you know what it feels like. And try to put your arms around it so you know how big or small it is.
Then your partner will take you back to where you started, remove your blindfold, and ask you to point out the tree! Can you remember which tree it was? Good job explorer!

Two more fun activities for you:

Try becoming a junior reporter! Here's how: Check out some newspapers and see if you can find any stories about trees, deforestation or a sickness that affects trees. It can be school newspapers or even listening to the radio. Did you hear anything important? Is anybody trying to help?

If you were a real reporter on TV, what would you say or do to help? Come up with some ideas!

And finally, would you like to build a tree house?
That is a fun project to do! Ask someone if they can help you to build one and share your ideas with others. *Remember:* Sharing is caring!

I hope you enjoyed this book on **Beautiful Trees** and always remember…

"Educating the mind without educating the heart is no education at all." - Aristotle

Author Bio

K. Bennett loves to write for both children and adults. Many different subjects are interesting to develop, but writing for children is special to her heart.

Her favorite pastimes include reading, traveling and discovering new things. Each of these activities helps to fuel her imagination and acts like a blank canvas waiting for more stories.

She is intrigued with fantasy elements like hidden worlds and faraway lands. And basically anything that gets her imagination soaring to new heights!

Her writing credits include children books online and other writing works listed at Amazon.com

Our books are available at

1. Amazon.com

2. Barnes and Noble

3. Itunes

4. Kobo

5. Smashwords

6. Google Play Books

Publisher

JD-Biz Corp

P O Box 374

Mendon, Utah 84325

http://www.jd-biz.com/

Mendon Cottage Books

P O Box 374, Mendon Utah 84325

www.ingramcontent.com/pod-product-compliance
Lightning Source LLC
Chambersburg PA
CBHW050844290526
45792CB00002B/513